The Power of Coaching

Volume 1

Inspiring Untold Stories for Business Growth and Life Transformations

D1329406

Compiled By Dr. Heather Tucker

CEO/Founder of www.AnotherLevelLiving.com and
www.AnotherLevelPublishing.com

Get to Know the 12 Authors in this Book!

There's ONE Page online where you can access all the authors' website and special offers from this book to make it super easy for you to follow up and connect with them further.

Go to **www.PowerofCoachingBook.com** right now before you forget. For a list of authors and their chapters, turn to the Table of Contents Page.

Enjoy the Book!

Sincerely,

Dr. Heather Tucker Biz/Life Harmony Trainer, Speaker, Coach, and Author to Entrepreneurs who want to Stress Less, Strengthen Relationships, and Lead with More Energy and Ease so that they can create Time, Money, and Emotional Freedom.

Published by Another Level Living, Inc. and Another Level Publishing, PO Box 64, Painter, VA 23420. (757) 656 – 1797 www.AnotherLevelPublishing.com

DISCLAIMER AND/OR LEGAL NOTICES

While all attempts have been made to verify information provided in this book and its ancillary materials, neither the authors nor publisher assume any responsibility for errors, inaccuracies, or omissions and are not responsible for any financial loss by customers in any manner. Any slights of people or organizations are unintentional. If advice concerning legal, financial, accounting, or related matters is needed, the services of a qualified professional should be sought. This book and its associated ancillary materials, including verbal and written training, are not intended for use as a source of legal, financial, or accounting advice. You should be aware of the various laws governing business transactions or other business practices in your geographical location.

EARNINGS & INCOME DISCLAIMER

With respect to the reliability, accuracy, timeliness, usefulness, adequacy, completeness, and/or suitability of information provided in this book, Dr. Heather Tucker, Another Level Living, Inc., its partners, associates, affiliates, consultants, and/or presenters make no warranties, guarantees, representations, or claims of any kind. Readers' results will vary. All claims or representations as to income earnings are not to be considered as average earnings. This book and all products and services are for educational and informational purposes only. Check with your accountant, attorney, or professional advisor before acting on this or any information. Dr. Heather Tucker and/or Another Level Living, Inc. is not responsible for the success or failure of your personal or professional decisions relating to any information presented by D. Heather Tucker, Another Level Living, Inc., or company products/services.

Any examples, stories, reference, or case studies are for illustrative purposes only and should not be interpreted as testimonies and/or examples of what readers and/or consumers can generally expect from the information. Any statements, strategies, concepts, techniques, exercises, and ideas in the information, materials and/or seminar training offered are simply opinion and experience, and thus should not be misinterpreted as promises, typical results, or guarantees (expressed or implied).

ISBN: 979-8-9865070-0-2

PRINTED IN THE UNITED STATES OF AMERICA

Dedication

To those who may have difficulty finding their way, know that you are not alone and there is glory on the other side.

Your test is your testimony.

You are fearfully and wonderfully made and called for amazing things!

Enjoy reading this book because it was created with you in mind.

A special thank you to our family and friends who support our entrepreneurial endeavors. And a huge thank you to all the awesome authors of this book.

Table of Contents

Introduction

This book, *The Power of Coaching,* Vol. 1, is for you if you are ready to achieve total success in your personal and professional development. In this book, you will read stories from business and life coaches who have successfully facilitated transformations and growth for others and their own lives. The purpose of this book is to highlight coaching as a solid avenue for reclaiming the power of your life through trust, truth, and transformation.

Coaching is an invaluable method for healing and positive change that too few people know about. We are here to make it more known. Coaching is available for anyone who chooses to invest in creating a brighter future for themselves and their loved ones. The beauty of coaching is that it bridges the gap from where one is to where they desire to be in any area of life. Too often we can live our lives based on the terms of others and never fully step into our calling.

The 12 authors in this book share stories of hope and possibility to shift any life into one filled with purpose, passion, and prosperity. Coaching can produce rapid, lasting results and change easily. These authors share their definition of coaching, testimonies of transformations that they facilitated and experienced for themselves, and key strategies they use to support others to take charge of their life journey. Through these stories, you will find that the benefits of coaching are priceless.

This book is divided into two sections. The first section includes chapters that focus on Business and Life Transformations. If you are a business owner, then you know that your business is an extension of all that you are, and these chapters will support you in your business and life growth.

The second section includes chapters that focus on Self and Life Transformation. These chapters were created for those seeking to become a better version of themselves and to those around them. While reading this book, you might even be inspired and find that you have a calling to become a coach. Our company, Another Level Living Inc., teaches entrepreneurs the business of coaching and we would be honored to support you on your journey.

It is our wish that you receive many nuggets of gold from these stories and are inspired to follow your true life path.

Have you ever thought of being an author? This is just one of the books that we produce and publish at our company. Each year, we publish one to three books highlighting topics including coaching, stories of hope, caregiving, mindset, and business. We look for authors every year; business owners and entrepreneurs who want to share their stories and strategies for success. If you've been wanting to write a book yourself or be a part of a compilation book like this, please reach out to us online. Here is a webpage that talks about the books that we produce. New books show up as they happen. www.AnotherLevelPublishing.com

As an author of seven books myself, I can tell you being an author has changed my life. I have been booked on more speaking gigs. I feel more confident. I have attracted more clients from people who read my book. And all of it brings me more Biz/Life Harmony.

Finally, the authors in this book want to hear from you! Each author has given a link to their website, where you can learn more about them and get their free gifts. Please take advantage of their offerings and reach out to connect with those who resonate with you.

Contact us if you have any questions about the authors, this book, Another Level Living Coaching Services, Certification Programs, or being a part of future books.

Elevate Your Business & Life Chapters

Victory is Already Yours

By Dr. Heather Tucker

"The Only Constant is Change." ~Heraclitus

Tell us about yourself, your expertise, and your coaching niche.

I am Dr. Heather Tucker, the Founder and CEO of Another Level Living, Inc. It is the only professional training and coaching company that produces deep, powerful transformations for entrepreneurs worldwide who want to overcome great fear and stand fully in their power, unshakable so that they can master communication and relationships in both business and life with ease and grace. I am a master Biz/Life Harmony trainer, speaker, and coach. I guide my clients in achieving total success and victory by using easy strategies that support them in working smarter, stressing less, increasing energy, expanding their capacity to receive abundance, and strengthening their relationships.

Because I believe in the transformation that coaching can bring, I also certify life coaches and communication (mind) experts and have certified over four hundred life coaches to date. My primary areas of expertise include business building, technology harmony, authentic leadership, relationship restoration, and healing trauma / Post-Traumatic Stress (PTSD). I fully know that it is possible to heal the past, live more in the present, and have a bigger vision for the future. This is possible for anyone and everyone.

Tell us, what does coaching mean to you?

After being in the coaching industry for the last seven years, coaching for me is all about trust, truth, and transformation. Big picture, coaching is about bridging the gap from where someone is to where they want to be. Coaching means overcoming and breaking free from the current and past struggles that prevent one from making their dreams a reality. Often, the significant emotional events in our life become obstacles that lead us to become stuck, clouded, and see no way out. It is easy to become and feel hopeless and want to give up on the important things to us, including people, places, and things. Coaching is about supporting others by stepping into their empowerment, tapping into the natural gifts and resources, and taking charge of their power and life again.

Coaching is about creating a harmony that naturally inspires clients and all to whom they are connected in their environments. As a coach, I am simply the tour guide supporting the transformation and holding the client accountable as they step into the more extensive and best version of themselves. Once a client tells me what they want to achieve, I hold the space for them, proudly watching them walk into that reality and being their biggest cheerleader. The beauty of coaching is that it facilitates the client into fully stepping into their purpose, passion, and prosperity, unleashing their greatness to their world, and owning their uniqueness on the journey. The power of coaching is available for all so that we can experience heaven on earth.

What kind of problems do you solve? Can you tell us a bit about the process that you walk people through?

I solve all conflicts that prevent clients from fully living their purpose, passion, and prosperity. Our businesses, careers, relationships, health, finances, and living environments are all extensions of us. Usually, there are conscious and unconscious blocks in our mind, or heart wounds from our past that ignite negative emotions, including anger, sadness, fear, hurt, guilt, as well as limiting thoughts and beliefs, such as I am not good enough, that prevent us from unleashing our greatness and owning all that we are.

We do not attract what we want as much as we attract what we are. Those with significant emotional events from the past, such as being raised with trauma, abuse, and neglect (spiritually, mentally, emotionally, and/or physically), tend to attract a life of chaos (toxic relationships, work environments, health issues, etc). It often produces a feeling of wanting to give up thinking that life will always be this way. It leads to unwanted behaviors, fears, phobias, playing small, and creates glass ceilings that need to be shattered. Big picture, I guide the transformation of those who have dealt with (past) or dealing with (present) toxic, unhealthy situations and environments into happy, healthy, and healed ones so that they can fully live with purpose, passion, and prosperity with ease. We do this using a 3-step process:

- **Step 1: Lean In** - Cultivate Awareness. All change starts with awareness. The awareness of how the past has impacted the present, how the same patterns play out, and how underneath all the surface-level chaos is just a great fear of coming closer.

There is so much more to awareness. What are you tolerating, and what are you avoiding? How are you in the midst of the chaos?

- **Step 2: Let Go** - Be the change you wish to see. We cannot control how others are and what they do, no matter how much we want to. But we can control how we respond to them and how we operate. Being the change includes ultimate forgiveness of God, Self, and Others. It entails healing the past, living more in the present, and expanding your vision for the future. This is my favorite step because most people do not know how to let go. Being an expert in energy and emotions, I make this process rapid and straightforward.

- **Step 3: Leap Forward** - There is always hope. When I became calm amid the chaos (the eye of the storm), the chaos around me disappeared. All that is left is unconditional love, faith, wisdom, power, and strength, and it can radiate out through you to your loved ones, community, and world. Your love can heal all things. Your test is your testimony and is the exact thing that will lead you to your purpose, passion, and prosperity.

Do you have a story about a client and how they achieved success with your coaching? Please give details.

There are so many stories I could share. I tend to attract people who have gone through significant traumas of loss and conflict, preventing them from moving forward with ease. Many of them have faith but have lost heart and feel stuck. One story that comes to mind is Heidi; she was one of my first clients. Heidi was the wife of an Army Veteran who had many health challenges due to his military and life-related Post-Traumatic Stress. They had a blended family and both previous marriages.

Heidi spent many of her 25 years married, holding the space and the love for the entire family. She was the glue that held the family together. Not only was she an amazing wife and mom, but she also always created a career path for her success and her own fulfillment. Heidi was the light of the family, even in the midst of darkness. Whereas Heidi's colleagues thought she had it all, Heidi's home life was far removed from the happiness others saw in her. She was surrounded by people and felt so very alone because the one person (her husband) who was supposed to be there for her, wasn't. She felt not good enough, supported, loved, valued, and appreciated for all her hard efforts to keep this family afloat. This pulled at her emotions and energy, and she felt it was not safe to be herself.

When Heidi came to me, she was at the end of her rope. She had just found out that her husband had been cheating on her for two years, without her knowledge and in her face. She had held up this bubble of love for so long, and now it busted with devastation, betrayal, deceit, mistrust, and was emotionally taxing on her mind, body, heart, and soul. Heidi, like many people, struggled with impostor syndrome (i.e., how the world saw her was not how she felt inside).

Working with me for only a short time, Heidi was able to heal from losses of and in her family. I guided her through a process of taking the burdens off herself and giving them to God so that she could better hear God's voice of her over her voice and the voices of others.

She started to see God's hand covering the entire situation and experienced many miracles each day. She and her husband eventually divorced due to her husband's continued infidelity and reluctance to get help. Nevertheless, she was able to heal from the years of broken-heartedness and heaviness she experienced from abuse and neglect, reclaim her power and her energy in her life, and embraced a new way forward.

She created more harmony in her life and later attracted an ideal dream job and a new life partner who loves her for all that she is. She has more harmonious relationships with God, herself, and others, even those that wronged her. She is now making a significant impact on the lives of others, sharing her story, and letting others know that the best is yet to come. She has more love, joy, peace, faithfulness, kindness, and wholeness than she ever had before and is a light that shines beautifully for others to see and know that there is hope.

Did you go through the difficulties that you now help people with? Tell us about that and how it led you to become a coach?

Yes, absolutely. I have had my share of issues with relationships, especially intimate ones, with myself and God. I was always so good at business and career, but there was something about relationships that I could not figure out. Graduating with my Ph.D. at 27 and landing my dream job at 28, I seemed to have had it all in the world. Yet, inside, there was so much sadness and misery. For a long time, relationships were toxic, and it was easier to stay away and push people away than it was to become closer together. I buried myself in work, tolerated, and ignored being treated less than. I became so overwhelmed in life that I had a popping moment and shut down. I decided that my career, relationships, and health were not bringing me joy, and it was time to change that. I also saw so many around me who were struggling with similar things. It was not until I discovered coaching that I was able to pull back the layers and get to the core of my misery. There were things in my past that I never dealt with, even from childhood, which brought me internal conflict. Chaos internally attracted chaos externally.

The secret I learned that changed everything is that all my relationships are reflections of me. When I stopped listening and taking in other people's judgments and perceptions about me and paid more attention to what God says about me, I was able to fall in love with all that I am. It changed how I saw myself as well as how others saw me. I became calm, and all the chaos around me, too, became calm. With years of guiding others in their healing, I was also being healed and restored. It restored others around as well. I came from a very dark place, and now, there is so much more confidence, hope, inspiration, empowerment, abundance, prosperity, and blessings all around me 24/7. My life now just gets better and better every day. I know that if I have gone through these things and overcome them, anyone can. We do not have to have a great past to have a great future, and we can restore and recreate ourselves each new day.

If someone were fearful of coaching, what would you tell them?

There is nothing to fear but fear itself. Most people, especially those who have experienced trauma, see fear as "Forget Everything and Run." This can only take us so far. It is so much easier to run and avoid pain. If we do not heal from what hurt us or is unconsciously blocking us, we will bleed all over those who do not deserve it. We will lose out and push away the very things that God wants to bless us with. Hurt people, hurt people, and healed people, heal people. Coaching provides a safe, confidential, and judgment-free zone where it is safe to be you, express what is going on, feel heard and acknowledged, heal, and act on the steps that you produce for the way forward. What we resist persists, and small problems become big mountains if we do not address them. Coaching allows you to redefine fear for yourself to easily "Face Everything and Rise" so that you can "Feel Everything and Relax." Breakthroughs and blessings happen much faster with coaching.

What would you tell someone that thinks they should be able to fix/solve this on their own?

Often, when we try to solve or fix something on our own, we start with good intentions and actions towards achievement, and then we fall off and go back into our regular patterns and behaviors. The beauty of coaching is the accountability, identifying and breaking through blocks as they arise to move forward with making permanent lasting changes on your own. Going the battle alone, you feel alone and that no one understands how you feel. Having support lets you know that you got this, and you are covered, even when it seems dim. Just reach out and try it; you will be so glad that you did!

How has being a coach and guiding others to empowerment influenced and changed your life?

Being a coach has transformed all areas of my life. I now see others and myself the way God does. I can see how the conflicts and woes of life weigh people down and drain their energy and I can easily hold the space for their mind, body, and soul freedom if they choose to break free. My empathy and communication for those around me have expanded to limitless levels. I have been able to positively influence and naturally impact others around me just by my presence alone and by being the change that I wish to see in the world. My life is now stress-free and full of ease, grace, and aloha. My mind, body, and soul feel at least ten years younger than me. I am excited about all that life offers and look forward to living my elderly years.

What would you tell someone who may have a calling to be a coach?

Coaching is the most beautiful calling someone could have. It creates wins all around for both the client and coach. It gives purpose, passion, and prosperity to all. It leads to more than coaching: speaking, authorship, and teaching, are just a few paths.

I hear two things from people who have a calling as a coach: "People always come to me for advice" and/or "I see so much happening in the world, and I want to help others." There are only two things needed to be a coach: a strong desire to help others and a willingness to grow and become a better version of yourself each day. If this sounds like you, let us chat!

Are there a few steps or tips you can give someone right now to start them on their transformation?

You are the captain of your ship and the master of your fate. Your healing is in your hands. It is easy to blame others for your situations. I challenge you to take charge of your life and not go the battle alone. Seek the right support that will be the biggest cheerleader in your transformation to a better life. You have a calling in your life and a purpose. It is time to live it, and I promise that your life can transform into all the amazement you are destined to experience. Victory is already yours if you choose to walk in it. The one bible verse that my grandma would always put in my cards is the very thing that led to all the greatness I have created with my company. Proverbs 3:5-6, "Trust in the Lord with All of Your Heart. Do not rely on your own understanding. In all your ways, acknowledge Him, and He will make your path straight."

Do you have a gift/session that you can offer us?

I want to offer you a free guide on *5 Secrets to Your Ultimate Business/Life Harmony.* Even if you are not in business, you can still benefit from this guide. I also want to offer you a one-on-one clarity call with me. Simply go to **www.AnotherLevelLiving.com** to access your gift and session.

About the Author

Dr. Heather H. Tucker

Dr. Heather is the Founder and CEO of Another Level Living, Inc. It's the only professional training and coaching company that produces deep, powerful transformations for entrepreneurs worldwide who want to overcome great fear and stand fully in their power, unshakable, so that they can master communication and relationships in both business and life with ease and grace. She is a master Biz/Life Harmony trainer, speaker, and coach. Dr. Heather guides her clients in achieving total success and victory by using easy strategies that support them in working smarter, stressing less, increasing energy, expanding capacity to receive abundance, and strengthening all their relationships. She also certifies life coaches and communication (mind) experts and has certified over 400 life coaches to date. This led her to create a community called the Aloha Mastermind: An Ohana (Family) for Coaches and Practitioners. Dr. Heather's primary areas of expertise include business building, authentic leadership, relationship restoration, and healing trauma / Post-Traumatic Stress (PTS).

Live Your Best Life

By Dr. Linda Jordon

Tell us about yourself, your expertise, and your coaching niche.

I am Dr. Linda R Jordon, wife, mother, and breast cancer survivor. After 27.5 years in corporate and surviving cancer, I started my own coaching & consulting business. As a business consultant/coach & trainer, I work with organizations, business owners, and professional leaders, helping them identify and close gaps in the workplace by setting goals and creating a strategy to increase productivity and growth in the workplace. I also provide and conduct leadership assessments and consult on performance management. As a diversity and inclusion trainer/consultant, I support organizations in facilitating diversity, equity, inclusion, and belonging training. I conduct organizational assessments, harassment training, and employee engagement surveys as part of the training program.

Tell us what does coaching mean to you?

Coaching is all about helping the individual and the organization and supporting their needs. It is essential to set aside dedicated time for each coaching client. You want to focus only on your client during this time...no phone calls, no checking emails, or anything else that should distract you from your client.

When coaching an individual, your objective is to listen more and talk less. Coaching is designed to ensure that everyone has the right tools, guidance, and information to assist them in having a clear and meaningful conversation and having clear actions as part of their development process.

Asking good questions and listening is the key to having a good coaching conversation. Coaching is not telling the individual what to do or say. Coaching is not about asking closed-ended questions that do not allow individuals to express themselves. Coaching is not about you doing all the talking...coaching is about listening.

What kind of problems do you solve? Can you tell us a bit about the process that you walk people through?

In coaching, my goal is to help the client solve the problem they bring forward during a session. My process follows the 3-step formula:

- **Step 1 - Create clarity:** I always start by asking the client how I can help them today or what areas they would like to focus on today. I then identify the issue or topic of discussion. During the conversation, I will ask, what is the outcome you are looking for?

- **Step 2 - Generate options:** After the client has shared the topic and provided specifics about the issue, I ask them what other options they have to solve the problem. I also want to know if these options are possible and what obstacles they perceive may come their way.

- **Step 3 - Move to action:** During this step, I want the client to share what plans or actions they are doing to do. I want them to provide details such as what is the timeframe for taking action. I also want the client to share how they plan to take action and share what success will look like for them. It is helpful to the client to be able to visualize success which always helps to motivate them to take action.

Do you have a story about a client and how they achieved success with your coaching? Please give details.

One of my clients struggled with work-family balance while trying to make a career change. The client was dedicated to their corporate job but had a deep desire to pursue their own business to help people. The client struggled with timelines, finances, social media and other tools, commitment to the new venture, dedication to the 9-5 job, and just managing life in general. Over a period of 6 months, the client and I worked on specific areas to help them get to their desired state. We first focused on what was their immediate need to feel some sense of relief in this transition. That first task was on timelines and scheduling. Like most of my clients, people have challenges with too much being on their work calendar and personal calendar. Yes, it takes a lot of time to get it all done. I always ask my clients what is keeping them up at night. Typically, that is where we start.

Helping my clients focus on scheduling, using a calendar, and staying committed to what is on the calendar made a huge difference for them. Initially, it was not easy for them to stay with the calendar and not deviate; however, consistency paid off. The client was able to focus on corporate work items during the day, have time for family after work and then set aside a few hours in the evening to focus on their dreams after corporate.

Did you go through the difficulties that you now help people with? Tell us about that and how it led you to become a coach?

While working in corporate, I did experience similar difficulties that my clients have faced. I started working in the corporate world in my early 20s. As a female of color, I always felt that I had to work harder and do more to be seen and heard. When I first started in corporate, I had not finished my undergraduate degree due to a lack of funding. So, I found a job hoping that this would help me pay off some bills and go back to college. Well, that did not work out as planned, so I kept working. I loved my job, the pay was OK at the time, but I wanted more.

Without a college education, I was limited in what I could do, so I applied for and completed my Bachelors in Business Administration. I thought having a degree would surely get me over any hurdles I might encounter. Yes, having a degree was helpful to a point. When I wanted to progress in my career and move into leadership, I was faced with obstacles such as not having enough experience and not having a master's degree. So, I then applied for and completed a Masters in Organizational Change & Leadership. This time, having a master's degree helped a great deal. I was able to move up in the organization; however, I still faced challenges. Again, being the only person of color in leadership in my area was difficult. Balancing work and life while having a career can be very demanding. I had to figure out what my priorities are.

Some additional challenges were, I would receive feedback such as...I did not talk enough in leadership meetings, I was too aggressive, or my expressions were not received well, I didn't show I cared, and I didn't share more about myself and my personal life. At this point, I felt like it was a no-win situation. So, I asked for a coach and attended various leadership trainings. I wanted to fix whatever was not working.

My coach helped me see that I was a little wound up too tight because I wanted to be perfect as a leader, mom, and wife. I was trying to manage and juggle all three in hopes that I would be seen as someone who could handle a senior leadership role. After several years of coaching and then becoming a mentor to others, I realized that I wanted to be a coach so that I could help others that faced similar obstacles and challenges.

If someone were fearful of coaching, what would you tell them?

Fear is a state of mind. There is nothing to be fearful of when it comes to coaching if that is what you desire to do. Everyone experiences fear, and it comes in three forms: fear of failure, fear of rejection, and I am not good enough. The fear of failure pops in our head when we are trying to lose weight; we do not want to let ourselves down or when we want to venture into a new career. That fear of failure makes us think we will not be successful doing something different. Fear of rejection gets in the way in similar situations. The fear of I am not good enough, not smart enough, or not tall enough...whatever your fear, it comes from the feeling of shame. You are now allowing yourself to be seen by others. You are comparing yourself to others when you should not be. Everyone has a gift or talent. Yes, someone will be better at a skill than you are, and that is OK. But remember, you have a skill that no one else has, which makes you special. Do not allow fear to hold you back from your greatness.

What would you tell someone that thinks they should be able to fix/solve this on their own?

Everyone would like to believe that they can solve their own problems. However, most of us cannot. When we try to solve our own problems, we start off well, and then we get distracted or become too personally attached to the situation. Often, we think we can tackle something better than someone else because we know it and understand it. Unfortunately, I am here to tell you that it does not work that way. We all must have a coach, a mentor, or some form of support to help us fix our problems. Doing things in a silo and solo is not healthy and not profitable.

How has being a coach and guiding others to empowerment influenced and changed your life?

As a coach, I can connect and reach people I would never think possible. I have connected with people from across the US and abroad through networking. Being able to communicate with others brings me great joy. I can learn about others, their lifestyles, their struggles/challenges, and what makes them excited about life.

Being a coach is more than just helping someone reach their goals and objectives or helping them to dig deep and find their power.

Coaching is about building a relationship with that person, building trust, and building a friendship. Coaching has allowed me to learn more about myself as I learn more about others. Each time I meet with a client, I learn one thing about myself, which helps me improve as a coach and improve personally.

What would you tell someone who may have a calling to be a coach?

Coaching is becoming a more popular business in recent years. Everyone needs coaching in some form or fashion. If you want to become a coach, I recommend that you first understand the difference between coaching, counseling, and mentoring. Oftentimes, people think these are the same. If you want to tell other people what to do, then I would suggest you become a mentor and help those who need mentoring.

If you are looking to help guide a person to greatness and help them fulfill their goals and objectives, then coaching is for you. Becoming a coach requires a few skill sets: listening, listening, and more listening. If you are someone who can ask great questions, keep the client focused, help the client improve their skills, and raise their competence, then coaching is for you. As a coach, you must believe that your client has all the answers to their situation within them. Your job as a coach is to extract those answers from them and help your client unlock their potential to illuminate that potential and live their best life.

Do you have a gift/session that you can offer us?

Yes, I am offering a FREE 30-minute Discovery Call to Illuminate Your Potential as well as my FREE eBook entitled Elevation of the Mind. Simply go to **www.LindaJordon.com** to access your free gifts.

About the Author

Dr. Linda R. Jordon

Dr. Linda R Jordon is a leadership consultant & personal development coach focusing on diversity and inclusion and organizational change management. Dr. Jordon has over 30 years of experience in management, leadership development & training, leadership coaching, business process improvement, diversity, and inclusion, contact center development & management, organizational development, and training within the U.S. and abroad.

As a leadership coach, Dr. Jordon works with business owners and professional leaders, helping them identify and close gaps in the workplace by setting goals and creating a strategy to increase productivity and growth in the workplace. Dr. Jordon has assisted with leadership assessments and performance management.

As a diversity and inclusion trainer/consultant, Dr. Jordon supports organizations in facilitating diversity and inclusion training. She has assisted with organizational assessments, harassment training and employee engagement surveys.

Coaching Saves Lives

By Kimberly Koste

Tell us about yourself, your expertise, and your coaching niche.

I am Kimberly Koste, MA, speaker, and social media attraction & relationship marketing coach. I help solopreneurs, and home-based business owners navigate the choppy waters of social media marketing and master the mindset necessary to get visible, get leads, and get paid!

Tell us, what does coaching mean to you?

Whether it is business, relationship, life, or sports, coaches teach, train, observe, correct, guide, encourage, push growth, keep accountability, and hold the highest vision for clients by asking intuitive, introspective questions that draw wisdom out of the client rather than preaching or telling clients what to do. Relationships are everything, and everything is a relationship. We cannot survive, much less thrive alone. I also think humans need objective perspectives to make informed decisions, support to "take the leap" oftentimes, and accountability so they can stay on track, make progress, and not fall into old patterns and habits that keep them from growing and achieving.

None of us are experts at everything. Therefore, we also need to share wisdom. In fact, that is what makes up a tribe. I see coaching as an extension of this healthy, interdependent human survival need. And coaching saved my life. Five years ago, I was fifty and heartbroken. "Is this seriously my life?" I thought. *That guy* dumped *me?* It was a huge wake-up call.

I immediately turned to coaching to heal my heart and get my certification. I had been introduced to coaching years before and was so impressed by its future-focused, "get 'er done" approach, that I knew immediately I wanted to be a coach.

Instead, I got a divorce and put it on the back burner for many years. But five years ago, with my heart broken wide open, I took the plunge before I could change my mind (i.e., listen to those pesky voices of limiting beliefs).

What kind of problems do you solve? Can you tell us a bit about the process that you walk people through?

I teach entrepreneurs how to better utilize the social media they are already on, to get leads for their business via organic audience growth, authentic relationship development, and amazing content that shows who they are as a whole person, ready to serve. I also teach them how to find their brand voice and create awesome content that gets engagement, which naturally attracts their ideal clients and customers, so they do not have to "find" them or chase them down.

So many entrepreneurs know they can and should use social media for business but have no idea what that means or where to start. "What do I post?" "When do I post?" and "Why do I post?" are questions I often hear. And I have been there. But like a foreign language, once you speak it, it is so fun and easy! But we do not learn overnight. So, I help people either one-on-one or in groups so they can choose what works for them. I also offer a membership for those who want the information dripped over time at a comfortable pace. Further, people love the community, and the membership is a beautiful place to have, find and create that.

In my membership, I help clients with the following problems:
- Mindset (we cannot do anything when fear is driving the bus)
- Content (what, where, when, how, why?)
- Feedback (from peers and ideal clients on what is working/not working)
- Community (nothing like having a ready group with whom to network and collaborate)

I also provide monthly training and get chills when I teach clients things they never knew, setting their business afire! Being our authentic selves, getting leads and making sales are what attraction marketing and my membership are all about.

Do you have a story about a client and how they achieved success with your coaching? Please give details.

Marie came to me wondering why a friend of hers was posting herself drinking her "green shot" every morning. In other words, "What am I missing?" When I told her not to post about her products, she confusedly said, "How will people know what I do then?"

Now, Marie understands the why and how of posting and that it is all about building a connection with the reader by being engaging enough to stop them from scrolling and comment. "Kimberly used examples and explained the process and purpose of good content and engagement in a simple manner that was easy to understand, including examples, and now, it all makes sense."

Did you go through the difficulties that you now help people with? Tell us about that and how it led you to become a coach?

I was a relationship coach for three years when I stumbled upon attraction marketing simply because it was suggested to me as a way to "get leads." I fell in love with it immediately. Meeting new people every day, making new friends, clients, and viewers? Hell, yes. I loved it so much that I left relationship coaching to teach others the language of attraction marketing.

Being an entrepreneur requires A LOT of mindset shifts, however, so I have kept that portion of my relationship coaching, which was more like fear busting and personal growth, anyway. Therefore, I feel totally aligned in my business right now.

If someone were fearful of coaching, what would you tell them?

There is nothing better (or easier) than having a guide show you exactly what you need to know or learn. Many coaches have different levels of access and teaching, so you can usually find your right price point.

What would you tell someone that thinks they should be able to fix/solve this on their own?

I might first ask, "How's that worked out so far?" The best of the best in their fields, whether it be sports or authors or other coaches, all have coaches. There is no "done" when it comes to learning, growing, or becoming better at something. I believe everyone needs coaching and should always have one on call for life's ups and downs.

We were not meant to thrive or even survive on our own. Humans need humans. We need each other and coaches for their objectivity, training, accountability, expertise, encouragement, and tough love. These things allow us to do things we will not do when left to our own devices, step out of our comfort zones and have the courage to try new things.

How has being a coach and guiding others to empowerment influenced and changed your life?

I have been a coach for five years. There is nothing better than seeing others learn something they did not know and have it transform their business, mindset, or life. I love to see clients soar, have an "ah-ha!" or experience a significant (or minor) breakthrough.

But more than being a coach, what changed my life is being coached. Being able to let go while someone else takes the lead is a gift. Not having to have all the answers, to be able to pick up the phone and ask someone else to help you work through a problem, is gold.

What would you tell someone who may have a calling to be a coach?

If you have a calling to be a coach, begin with sales training. Marketing yourself is the hardest part. Putting a price on your value brings up all kinds of barriers. Get a great coach who can work with you on mindset and teach you how to sell before you do anything else. This is the most significant area of personal growth you will experience and the hardest. You might as well start here and "get it over with." Everything after that, finding your niche, nailing your messaging, deciding what kind of coach you want to be will all flow after this.

Are there a few steps or tips you can give someone right now to start them on their transformation?

Transformation requires a few mindset shifts. Nothing changes if nothing changes, and it starts with "me."

1. **Step into a new identity**. So often, it is over-identifying with some part of ourselves that keeps us from changing. "I'm a night owl," for example, can make it hard to get up early when necessary. To lose weight, one might have to step into the identity of someone who NEVER (okay, rarely) skips workouts, who eats "on plan" 98% of the time, and stops drinking wine every night. So, who do you need to BE to see change?

2. **Set an intention (not wish) and visualize in DETAIL what you will create.** Using all five senses and visualizing often can help you gain clarity and bring things to fruition. Setting an intention will help you make decisions. Does this take me one step closer to my intention or not?

3. **Optimize your environment**. Sometimes there are people in our lives holding us back. Sometimes it's the wrong job. Make sure you have the support you need, and the environment set for success.

4. **Always be working on personal development**, reading, watching, or listening to successful people who have "figured it out" and helped others is KEY.

Do you have a gift/session that you can offer us?

Optimize your social media for business by making a few small tweaks in my FREE Facebook Facelift session. A few small changes to your profiles can make you pop, and we'll talk about how to easily tweak your content for more engagement, too! To access your session, simply go to my website: **www.KimberlyKoste.com**

About the Author

Kimberly Koste

Kimberly Koste, MA is a speaker and attraction marketing and mindset coach. She teaches home-based entrepreneurs the language of social media marketing and shows them how to have FUN building their audience.

Her clients learn to leverage the social media they are already using to get more leads, create engaging content, and build an audience ready to follow them to the ends of the earth, in a heart-centered, organic, and authentic way.

Kimberly also helps her clients develop their marketing mindset. Speaking in front of people, getting visible and generally "putting yourself out there," can be tough for a lot of people. She loves to help her clients break through fears and get fast results with her direct, no judgment approach, and by infusing fun!

Face Everything and Rise

By Dr. Sunny Fridge

Tell us about yourself, your expertise, and your coaching niche.

I am a New York girl living in a Mississippi world. I am an award-winning professional speaker, entrepreneur, and communication coach. I earned a doctorate in urban higher education in 2007 from Jackson State University. I received my master's degree in public communications from Fordham University and a bachelor's degree in communications from the College of New Rochelle. I have received several certifications, including certified coach with the Maxwell Leadership team, eSpeakers Certified Virtual Trainer, and most recently certification as a Roger Love Method Speaking Coach. Over the past 20 years, I have mentored and coached hundreds of students and clients to help them develop skills to become successful communicators and leaders. As the owner of Sunny Fridge Consulting, LLC, my passion is helping others to unleash their untapped potential through workshops, seminars, and coaching. My niches are communication, leadership, and presentation skills coaching.

Tell us, what does coaching mean to you?

I believe coaching is a "calling." I am passionate about the opportunity to help a client get from where they are, to where they want to be. Coaching helps individuals unlock their potential to become the next best version of themselves as they achieve a goal. A goal is anything you desire to experience, create, get, do, or become. At the end of the day, my clients want to become more confident as speakers, entrepreneurs, or leaders. I help them get clarity about the fears, distractions, or obstacles that keep them from reaching their goals. Although I'm a teacher at heart, as a coach, I help clients learn best by asking questions as I guide them through the coaching process.

What kind of problems do you solve? Can you tell us a bit about the process that you walk people through?

As a presentation skills coach, I help shy speakers, entrepreneurs and rising leaders overcome fear to speak with confidence and ease. I do this through workshops, one-on-one and group coaching. My structured approach helps people overcome their speaking fears while nurturing the confidence that comes from practicing. My coaching style is results oriented. My process involves helping clients understand what fear is so they can take action to have the desired transformation.

I facilitate a free monthly Confident Speakers Workshop to help participants feel both comfortable and confident when they step into a public speaking situation. Before the end of my workshop, I offer attendees the opportunity to continue working on their communication skills by becoming coaching clients. I first have a discovery call to make sure we both agree we are a great fit for each other. Before our first session, I have them sign a coaching contract. A contract offers accountability because it outlines what both parties expect during the sessions. My public speaking clients also complete a public speaking fears assessment. I also have a pre-session plan for my clients to help them focus and stay present during our session.

Do you have a story about a client and how they achieved success with your coaching? Please give details.

One of my favorite coaching moments was with a client who was dealing with self-confidence issues. She worked as a financial advisor with mostly male colleagues whom she felt did not take her seriously. She hated giving presentations. Her fear of making mistakes, forgetting what she was going to say, or wondering whether people would listen to her caused her significant anxiety. During our sessions, I helped her find her voice, craft her message, and hone her delivery. After my sessions, she gave her first presentation and the audience loved her talk. It was a real confidence booster for my client to develop the courage and mindset to believe in herself and her abilities. She shared with me that the coaching process was life changing. Her transformation was priceless!

Did you go through the difficulties that you now help people with? Tell us about that and how it led you to become a coach?

I had been living my dream as an educator at a local university for 15 years in the Communications department. In 2015, there were leadership changes. My contract was not renewed. Suddenly, I was no longer teaching and training students to be reporters, producers, or communicators. It was a difficult time in my life. I experienced fear and doubt. My confidence plummeted. But as my colleague Dr. Willie Jolley says, "A setback is a setup for a comeback!" I did what I had always encouraged my students to do. I began to dream big! I joined Toastmaster's International, an organization that helps individuals develop their communication and leadership skills in a supportive environment. In 2016, I became a John Maxwell certified coach, speaker, and trainer. I was mentored and coached by world-class faculty, which empowered me to start a consulting and coaching business. Most recently, I co-founded Speak & Shine Academy to empower kids and adults to unleash their speaking superpowers. And the rest, as they say, is history.

If someone were fearful of coaching, what would you tell them?

If you have goals you want to achieve or an obstacle you want to overcome, working with a coach is a great way to get the clarity you need to succeed. Once you realize you can trust your coach, you will find that your session is a safe space to talk about some of the self-limiting beliefs holding you back. The negative emotions you may feel will subside as you take action toward your goal. I truly believe having a coach is one of the best investments you will make in your personal and professional growth journey.

What would you tell someone who thinks they should be able to fix or solve this on their own?

Many people never have a coach, and they still succeed in life. But they often get stuck at various stages of their journey. That is where the power of coaching comes in. Think about athletes. For example, Michael Jordan did not become one of the greatest of all-time basketball champions by himself. He had coaches and lots and lots of practice. No matter what your career is, more than likely, a coach can help you become aware of your strengths and help you address the weaknesses as you set goals.

How has being a coach and guiding others to empowerment influenced and changed your life?

I am reminded of a quote by Oprah Winfrey, "There is no paycheck that can equal the feeling of contentment that comes from being the person you are meant to be." I never get tired of feeling the contentment when I help someone achieve aha moments and transformation. It reminds me that I am fulfilling my purpose and doing what I was born to do. Before I became a coach, I used to only think about achieving success. Since becoming a coach, I also think about achieving significance. I think about the positive impact I can make in the lives of others. It is a joy to see my clients achieve goals and reach milestones they never thought were possible. I love helping an entrepreneur get clarity on their message for their new business venture or helping a parent become a better communicator in relationships with their spouse or children. It is rewarding to empower a rising leader to get unstuck and gain new perspectives that lead to a promotion or dream job. I feel so blessed to be able to make a living while making a positive difference in the world, one coaching client at a time!

What would you tell someone who may have a calling to be a coach?

Since the pandemic, the business of coaching has skyrocketed. If you think you have a calling to be a coach, make sure you also have a coach. And make sure you have a personal growth plan so that you can be the best version of yourself as you help others achieve success as they become the best version of themselves.

Are there a few steps or tips that you can give someone right now to start them on their transformation?

One of the first things I learned from my coach is that values drive goals. To get started on your transformation, I want you to take a few minutes to list three to six of your core personal values. These are important to you and how you live your life. Values help you determine the difference between what is good or bad for you, helpful or a hindrance, essential or insignificant for your way of life. No answer is wrong. There are many values ranging from trust, faith, and family to independence and balance. I often say, "You've got to know yourself to grow yourself." Knowing your core personal values help you decide your priorities and goals as you work with your coach on living your best life.

Do you have a gift/session that you can offer us?

I am happy to offer my course, 7 Day e-Coach: A Step-by-Step Plan for Living Your Life like It's Golden. This online course is for you if you have ever asked yourself, "What are my unique gifts and talents?", "How do I develop them?", Or "What do I fear the most when it comes to living my dream?" Access your gift on my website: www.SunnyFridge.com

About the Author

Dr. Sunny Fridge

Sunny Fridge, Ph.D. (aka Dr. Sunny) is a New York girl living in a Mississippi world. She is an award-winning professional speaker, educator, and entrepreneur. Dr. Sunny is a Certified Virtual Presenter and a certified coach, speaker, and trainer with the John Maxwell Team.

As a presentation skills coach, her mission is to help camera-shy speakers, entrepreneurs, and rising leaders overcome fear to speak with confidence and ease, so they can share their message with the audience they are called to serve.

Dr. Sunny is committed to educating, mentoring, and supporting other entrepreneurs. Keeping in line with that commitment, she founded Chance Network, a non-profit venture to empower young people and women through professional development workshops, webinars, and coaching. As co-founder of Speak & Shine Academy, she teaches public speaking to kids and youth. She is coach of two Speak & Shine Youth Clubs run by members, who practice their communication and leadership skills in a fun and supportive environment.

Make Your Dreams Come True

By Nancy Matthews

"To the world, you may be one person; but to one person, you may be the world." ~ Dr. Seuss

Tell us about yourself, your expertise, and your coaching niche.

Nancy Matthews, Leadership, Marketing and Sales. The central focus of my coaching is about PEOPLE – who you are, whom you serve, how you serve, and how you can be "The One" for yourself and others. When you focus on people first and how you can be "The One" for them, your life and business flourish.

Tell us, what does coaching mean to you?

Coaching is an opportunity to receive new perspectives so that you can reach your desired goals with greater ease and flow.

What kind of problems do you solve? Can you tell us a bit about the process that you walk people through?

I do a combination of business coaching and personal development coaching. People come to me when they have hit some type of "wall" in getting the results they want. I begin by asking a series of questions to uncover where the block or blind spot is and then support them in reframing the challenge so they can move forward.

My uniqueness comes from my personal experiences and my combined skill set of understanding human behavior in relation to business and personal life. Plus, I am quite the tech geek and can show entrepreneurs how to bust through challenges when it comes to marketing themselves so that they can have a more significant impact and earn more income.

Do you have a story about a client and how they achieved success with your coaching? Please give details.

Stacey was a relationship coach who wanted to take her business to the next level. She had kept her prices at the same rate for years and had hit a wall with how to earn more money and serve more people. By working together to uncover her own limiting beliefs and create a new belief system, she was able to raise her prices, confidently ask for and be paid those higher prices.

Did you go through the difficulties that you now help people with? Tell us about that and how it led you to become a coach?

Oh yes! I have had my fair share of challenges. From being a single mom, starting my own business, and dealing with issues of unworthiness; it has been quite the journey to the woman I am today. I "fell" into coaching when more and more people began asking, "Nancy, how did you do it?" It being ... become a successful real estate investor, build several businesses, learn to stand on my own and escape abusive relationships, keep a positive attitude in the face of adversity (and the list goes on and on). In my desire to be of the highest value and service to people, I became an avid student of human behavior and share what I have learned with others so that they can move forward more easily and rapidly in their business and in their lives.

If someone were fearful of coaching, what would you tell them?

First, I would acknowledge that they feel fearful and seek to uncover what it is that they fear—being vulnerable? Being exposed? That they would receive bad advice? Once that is discovered, we can move forward in small steps to build trust in themselves and trust in me as their coach.

What would you tell someone that thinks they should be able to fix/solve this on their own?

"Great! How has that been working for you so far?" I would first acknowledge their desire to have different results and ask, "What do you think has prevented you thus far from achieving what you want?" Oftentimes, reluctance to coaching comes about because people feel uncomfortable asking for help. I would point out that collaborating with a coach is about helping you get further faster, avoiding some of the pitfalls already encountered and overcome.

How has being a coach and guiding others to empowerment influenced and changed your life?

Every day, I wake up filled with gratitude that this is my job. "Wow, I get to work with so many people who are up to great things, who want to be the best version of themselves and fulfill their potential as they positively impact the world."

What would you tell someone who may have a calling to be a coach?

As you embark on this rewarding – and sometimes challenging career, remember this: "You are responsible TO your clients, not FOR them." I gleaned this advice from my mentor, John Maxwell. It can be disheartening when you bring your best to a client, but they are still challenged, and you can see that if they would just apply what you have suggested, their lives would be so much better. Have patience, always be and do your best, and trust that the seed you planted will blossom when the time is right.

Are there a few steps or tips that you can give someone right now to start them on their transformation?

Begin by focusing on what you want. Often when people are desiring change, they know what they do not like but have not taken the time to focus on what it is that they do want. Observing your thoughts and language is a great first step in shifting your focus to what you would enjoy rather than focusing on all the things that aren't working. Keep track of every time you say something like:

- I cannot stand it when _____
- I do not like _____
- How come this always happens to me?
- Or other statements that are focused on why something is not working?

Then, for each statement, consider the contrast to what it is that you would prefer. What you focus on expands and as you shift your focus to what you would prefer rather than on what you do not want – you will get more of that.

Do you have a gift/session that you can offer us?

Yes, I'm offering my free audio on How to Create the Results You Want Without Hesitation or Frustration: Learn to Tune in to Your Intuition. You can access your gift on my website here: **www.NancyMatthews.com/Intuition**

About the Author

Nancy Matthews

Nancy Matthews is a Leadership, Sales & Marketing Expert, whose life, and work are grounded in one central theme, that is, that the most important things in life aren't things - life and business are about PEOPLE.

Her best-selling book, The One Philosophy: A Better Life for You and Humanity gives us a blueprint for valuing ourselves and others by treating every person you meet as "The One."

She is the Founder of The People Skills Academy and Co-Founder of Women's Prosperity Network.

Elevate Your Life & Self Chapters

Heal the Past and Free Your Soul

By Dorcas Richmond-David

"As soon as healing takes place, go out and heal somebody else."
~ Maya Angelou

Tell us about yourself, your expertise, and your coaching niche.

I am The Soul Freedom Coach. I specialize in coaching that frees the soul of negative ties that can hinder your path going forward. By creating and holding the place of grace, I can provide a pressure-free healing environment. My goal is to unburden the soul of emotional stressors, triggers, soul torment, and physical ailments that may be stealing your happiness. While unblocking the soul, not only will you feel hopeful excitement, but also the ability to mentally and physically make a change to move into your calling. As a Soul Freedom Coach and devoted Believer who has conquered many battles of suffering to set my soul free, I created a method of gently nudging others to step outside their comfort zone lovingly. I have used this method to assist many women to find their calling and live in a place of joy.

Tell us what does coaching mean to you?

Coaching gave me the ability to heal and move forward from a lot of grief in my life, while normal counseling did very little. I saw a licensed counselor for about a year after my husband's death. I liked her, she was good at her job, but I was looking for more. She helped me stop crying every day, but I could not find joy. About three years later, I found an excellent coach who helped me find joy and direction in a very short period. So having this experience of immense freedom in my soul, I set out to help free others.

What kind of problems do you solve? Can you tell us a bit about the process that you walk people through?

Every person is unique, and there is no one approach that fits all. I like to start by finding where they are in their life using several processes to gain this knowledge. The first time I went through one of these processes, my eyes were opened. I was surprised to learn that I thought I knew where I stood at that moment; however, I was only looking at the surface of my life. This lays the groundwork to help identify the areas you want to focus on or the issues you want to address that are causing trauma, blockage, triggers, and or stress in your life.

I have learned through my experience that if you don't address the underlying issues, you have had or are currently having, you can reach goals and still not experience true happiness. We all have baggage and trauma that we are living with the aftereffects. If you start by identifying where you are, where you want to go, WHAT is holding you back, and address them, you will be much happier and more fulfilled once you get there.

Do you have a story about a client and how they achieved success with your coaching? Please give details.

I have assisted many women at every age level to identify areas holding them back from their calling. One individual that comes to mind is a woman who had a child and married a man with three children. She went from being a single mom to a wife and mother of four. Talk about an overwhelming change in her life. She was excited about being a wife and looked forward to being a mother to more children since she loved children. Even though this was a new, exciting experience, she was weighed down and having trouble adjusting to so many life-changing events at once. She felt overwhelmed, defeated, angry, extreme fatigue, and felt the world was against her. She was lost and had no control over her emotions. We worked with the subconscious to find the core issues and soul wounds she struggled with. After working with me, she has found freedom, living with her emotions in check and living a life of peace and fulfillment. She is now connected to her family and the world around her and has gone on to impact many other women and children in finding their life callings.

Did you go through the difficulties that you now help people with? Tell us about that and how it led you to become a coach?

I was a PK (Preacher's Kid), so I grew up with not just one set of parents, but many, telling me what I should or should not do. One parent went so far as to call my father and tell him I should be best friends with his daughter and to make this happen. This caused me to have a lot of bitterness and anger, which I could not show.

On top of this bitterness, I experienced a lot of loss in my life, causing severe grief. I was very close to my father and lost him when I was

21. I married my soul mate and the love of my life. During our marriage, we experienced several miscarriages, more loss. In 2010 my husband Richard had what we thought was a heart attack but ended up that his heart exploded. We were blessed with a heart transplant, Richard lived well for four years, then I lost him in 2015. A couple of months later, I lost my dearest and closest Aunt on Richard's birthday. A few years later, I moved to Virginia, looking for a shorter winter and wanting to be by the beach. I loved the new town and being by the beach, but the joy still was not there.

One of my best friends of thirty-plus years was moving down, and we were going to start a business together that we had talked about for about twenty years. This idea was exciting, and I was looking forward to this new venture. She was starting to spend time looking for a house in the area, and we put money down on a building for the new business. A few months later, I lost her. Not only had I lost her, but also the dream of our new business.

I believe in God and Heaven, and I know all these people I have lost are in heaven. Without a doubt, they knew Jesus as their personal Savior. So, I was happy knowing I would see them again someday, but I had no joy in my life and found myself sad and crying a lot. I usually walk each morning for about an hour, and I found myself in a place where this hour was spent walking and crying. I sought out a counselor. She was good and helped me stop crying every day, but I could not find joy in my life.

I was on the brink with all this loss and built-up anger. I found a great coach and, soon after, started taking her classes. During this time, I learned that by addressing the subconscious mind through several processes and addressing the bound-up emotions, triggers, and other soul ties head-on, I was able to find joy once again. The other main thing I learned was that by using these new skills, you can work through trauma much more quickly and without a lot of rehashing the past, what a relief. My desire now is to assist, teach and empower other women to find true joy.

What would you tell someone that thinks they should be able to fix/solve this on their own?

I learned that I was able to give clients the space and tools to address their fears, anxiety, depression, and more. Eighty percent of our decisions and behavior come from our subconscious. Most people do not address the subconscious level, nor do they know how to. The modalities that I have learned through Another Level of Living teach you how to work with the subconscious and assist your clients in addressing the trauma that they did not even know was affecting them.

How has being a coach and guiding others to empowerment influenced and changed your life?

It is transforming to see clients' lives change. To see them be able to manage life with a more positive stride and find peace, joy, and move in the direction of their calling. Witnessing this transformation before your eyes is fantastic. I love seeing them living in a place of taking their lives back and knowing absolute joy sometimes for the first time in their lives.

What would you tell someone who may have a calling to be a coach?

Find a good Coach; all coaches need a coach themselves. Find a good program that is well-rounded. There are many programs with many claims; if you start by having them coach, you will know their style and know if what they teach aligns with your values.

Are there a few steps or tips that you can give someone right now to start them on their transformation?

One of the first things I learned from my coach that I continue to use today is a "Box Breathing" technique. It is a simple but profound process aimed to return breathing to its normal rhythm; even the Navy Seals use it. When I find myself in a stressful situation, I can do this for less than a minute and calm myself right down on the inside. At the time I learned about this, I had been walking around with a pain in my lower chest that was always there. It was there for years, and I was just used to it. Once I did a week of box breathing, three to four times a day, this pain went completely away and has not come back. You can find a great article on Medicinenet.com called "Why Do Navy Seals Use Box Breathing."

Do you have a gift/session that you can offer us?

Stop by **www.SoulFreedomCoach.com** to get a gift - Four points to set you on the path to set your "Soul" free. A one-time, 30-minute coaching session is available to see if we connect and if you feel I would be the right coach to lead you down the path to finding your peace, joy, and calling.

About the Author

Dorcas Richmond-David

Dorcas Richmond-David is the Soul Freedom Coach. We are a Spirit that lives in a Body that has a Soul. Our Souls can be affected through trauma from ourselves, others and events causing stress, anxiety, anger, fear, depression and more. Her great passion is bringing healing to people, so they can live in joy, have peace, and walk in their calling.

She knows that no one single approach is the right one for every individual person. Therefore, she has been trained in and continues to learn many modalities including (NLP - mind mastery), Integration of emotions, Living in Harmony, and Life Coaching. All of these give different ways to address trauma and to assist the individual into a harmonious lifestyle.

Trust the Process

By Milicent Hubert

"You are free to make whatever choice you want, but you are not free from the consequences of the choice." ~ Unknown

Tell us about yourself, your expertise, and your coaching niche.

After years of hating myself and hating life, I decided that I wanted to LIVE. I wanted to be free from past pain and emotional limitations that had been spoken and placed on my life. Your ugly, no one will ever love you, your dumb, and you will never achieve and be anything in life. These are some phrases that broke me! Well, today, I hear you are beautiful, I love you, you are so smart, and most importantly, I am me! Life Coach Milicent! I am Milicent Hubert, a wife, mother, grandmother, daughter, sister, and so much more. I am a Master Certified Life Coach and Certified Neuro-Linguistic Programming (NLP) Practitioner. My niche is helping women and teens find life harmony and heal from the inside out. Many times, we deal with trauma and turmoil, and that begins to take a toll on our health and emotions. I am here to help you heal and release so that you can have a more balanced life.

Tell us, what does coaching mean to you?

From a client standpoint, Coaching means being able to identify obstacles that are holding me back, clarify my goals and then come up with a strategic plan to help overcome those said obstacles. Being a Life coach means I get the opportunity to help motivate women and teens to achieve their personal goals and dreams. I get to offer a different way of thinking. Being non-judgmental provides a space of peace, calm, and safety. Bringing value to someone's life and helping seek balance in life as well as helping to understand their emotions.

What kind of problems do you solve? Can you tell us a bit about the process that you walk people through?

I solve problems dealing with feeling overwhelmed and feeling stuck in a situation, with traumas associated with emotional and mental limited beliefs and relationships. I focus on the whole person, mind, body, and soul. My process starts off with a few minutes of breathing to help clients relax. After we meditate, I ask, why are you here? I use this question to get the mind going and this allows me to go deeper. I also use the wheel of life method. This process will enable me to see areas that we will need to focus on. I give homework, which allows my clients to think more about the situation, which in turn allows me to go deeper into the situation as we find things throughout the week that will come up. I also allow time to deal with the stages of emotions and give comfort and understanding as we deal with the trauma. Throughout this process, I also share moments of life that helps my client become comfortable with me, which allows them to trust me.

Do you have a story about a client and how they achieved success with your coaching? Please give details.

I had a client that did not love life anymore. She was ready to "Throw in the towel." Her marriage was falling apart, and her children were completely out of control. She had lost herself trying to please everyone around her, except for herself. Dealing with the mental and physical abuse was just the beginning when we began to talk. At first, I was unsure I would be able to help her.

I looked at her and saw my younger self. I started by giving her positive affirmations for her to repeat daily. "I am smart, I am beautiful, and I am loved"! Building up her confidence and self-worth was my first goal, and we focused on just that for about a month. I understood that I would fail if we went any further without those two things being in place.

I scheduled a day of pampering as one of our sessions, so she would be able to share this moment with someone and help her to make positive memories. After she learned how to love herself, the next step was to focus on the other parts of her life. We began to deal with her marriage and why it was failing. One of the key reasons was that she did not know how to love because she did not know how to love herself, which is why self-love was the first step in working with her. Once we begin to work through those issues, many other components started to fall into place.

We were then able to focus on her relationships with her children. I had to have a session with her where we just dealt with her childhood to get her to a point where she could release all her past hurt and emotions and start her healing process. While healing, she began to see that her children were dealing with some of the same trauma she was trying to heal from, and they could heal together. Although her marriage ended, they could walk away as the best of friends. Her relationships with her children grew stronger, and they are doing well in life now. She has started dating and completely loving herself more every day.

Did you go through the difficulties that you now help people with? Tell us about that and how it led you to become a coach?

In life, I dealt with many traumas: domestic violence, verbal, mental, and emotional abuse, depression, suicidal thoughts, looking for love in all the wrong places, and becoming a teen mother.

Becoming a mother, I say, saved my life. I finally knew what unconditional love felt like. Although life did not get easier, I now had a reason to fight! I now had a reason to focus on my dreams and goals. I now had a reason to start loving myself! I knew I had to protect my son at all costs from all the things that I had experienced growing up. I was able to graduate high school with the help of my "angels" on earth. Although I was still dealing with a lot of limiting beliefs and all the abuse, I fought every day to try and be better. I fought every day to gain love from others, to be accepted as a friend because those were the things I still desired. Then God blessed me with my daughter! Another sign that He heard my cries. I still went through abuse, but it felt as each word was spoken, or with each hit I took, I began to become stronger and had a desire to fight, I decided I wanted to live!

I began to learn how to love myself. I started looking at myself through the eye of my children; I needed to see what they saw. I learned to love myself and embrace myself. Music was my therapy to heal. My faith gave me the strength to fight, and my children gave me a reason to live! Although I still had a way to go, I found love, and I found someone to love me just as I was.

I was able to seek and find help to break through all the walls I had put up around me to protect myself from hurt. I was able to deal with my childhood trauma. After going through this, I realized I had the knowledge and wisdom I wanted to share. After years of being the shoulder for individuals to cry, I learned about being a Life coach, and here I am today!

If someone were fearful of coaching, what would you tell them?

It is understandable to fear what you may not understand, being vulnerable to a stranger, or allowing someone to be vulnerable to you. Starting something new is always a fearful experience. Wondering if you will say something wrong or give the wrong advice. Just trust the process, fall back on your personal experiences and things you have learned through education.

What would you tell someone that thinks they should be able to fix/solve this on their own?

It is a challenging journey when you try to walk through the fire alone. Dealing with emotional pain alone is enough to break a person. There is not any shame in the stigma of seeking professional help. Someone that can see from the outside looking in. Sometimes we can get in our way because we cannot see beyond what is before us. It is ok to say, "I need help."

How has being a coach and guiding others to empowerment influenced and changed your life?

Being a life coach has tremendously changed my life. As I work with others, I reflect on how I dealt with the problems, and I learn and grow as well. I want to be able to offer the best version of myself to clients. To do so, I learn and expand my training constantly so that I can be the best for others.

What would you tell someone who may have a calling to be a coach?

I would say that every obstacle, every challenge, every up and down, good, or bad, that you have experienced in your life was not only for you but to help someone else. You came out of all of that to be able to bring someone else out. You have a gift and the ability to reach others that someone else may not be able to. Just cultivate your gifts and learn how to coach others through your experience.

Are there a few steps or tips that you can give someone right now to start them on their transformation?

A few steps that I can offer are:
1. Reflect on the things you want to change or solve.
2. Meditate and allow your mind and body to be at peace after taking a trip down memory lane.
3. Write down your emotions, just as you felt them.
4. Allow yourself to forgive. Forgive others, and most importantly, forgive yourself.

These simple steps will allow you to start a path of healing and live a more balanced life.

Do you have a gift/session that you can offer us?

Yes, I am offering a free clarity call and access to my free e-book, entitled, "7 Secrets to Overcoming Turmoil." Simply visit my website to access your gifts:

www.BreakthroughWithEmpowerment.com

About the Author
Milicent Hubert

Milicent Hubert is a Master certified Life and Wellness coach and a Certified NLP, who help women and teens to overcome emotional stress, mental and physical abuse. Being a survivor and learning how to trust and love again was a process that she did on her own. Now she would like to take her experience and coach other.

Before starting career as a life and wellness coach, Milicent worked in healthcare for over 13 years in claims and as a patient service coordinator and served as a mentor for youth with a non-profit organization. After having a successful career in healthcare and being a mentor, Milicent now finds joy in coaching women and teens on the process of healing from the inside out by focusing on mind, body, and soul.

Milicent enjoys spending time with her family and listening to music while relaxing. Milicent is the CEO and Master Life and Wellness Coach of Break Through with Empowerment LLC, where she offers group and one on one coaching sessions.

Harvesting Hope Through Trauma

By Nikki Richmond

Tell us about yourself, your expertise, and your coaching niche.

"I'm sorry to tell you, your newborn son has a very complicated form of heart disease and needs surgery immediately." Watching my son being taken from me, being a single first-time mother, these words echoed in my mind like a terrible dream. The long string of trauma following this determent would almost be the end of me...almost.

Hope seemed fleeting to me as my son went through each surgery only to find out he needed another. Then, I would soon meet the clutching grasps of grief for my mother, niece, uncle, and daughter. As I went through emotions and turmoil, God would soon show me the purpose in my pain. I would become a life coach specializing in trauma to assist countless others suffering and become living proof that you do not need a good past to have an awesome future. I do not just focus on the pain of trauma in my coaching, I guide my clients through an essential release process that leaves them feeling lighter and happier.

Tell us, what does coaching mean to you?

Raising a child takes a village! A big part of suffering comes from the feeling of not being supported. Life coaches are that necessary village for battling the villains of life. I often heard as a child, that everyone has problems; no one problem was greater than the other. At the time, I did not understand that although problems were supposed to be equal, the situations and stipulations were not. One person's problem may be easier for another person who has a better foundation of support, communication, understanding, and valuable resources. The best part about life coaching is that you do not have to be of a particular status to benefit from the endless knowledge and resources of coaching.

What kind of problems do you solve? Can you tell us a bit about the process you walk people through?

Problems I solve can have an overwhelming weight of emotions stemming from unresolved past issues, of which trauma plays a vital role. Previously, I lacked the support and tools that a life coach was able to show me with ease and grace. This impacted my life so positively, that becoming a life coach was important to my journey, as well as restoring happiness for others. Until being a certified life coach, I felt as though my personal journey was too difficult and painful to bear. As a child of therapy, I can remember the feelings after every therapist I had talked to, which was feeling on top of the world, followed quickly by feelings of hopelessness. What my treatment lacked was the ability to release dark and painful memories and focus on a new gloriously bright future. This is exactly what I do as a coach with my clients. I serve as a guide, cleansing and renewing minds and purpose with a feeling of hopeful excitement for a clear attainable future.

Do you have a story about a client and how they achieved success with your coaching?

Feeling inadequate almost held me back from coaching a dear friend who was silently suffering. After connecting, we found the root of each issue, my unique form of release turned out to be exactly what she needed to reignite the flame of hope inside her. We were able to establish what areas of her life needed more of her concentration, and able to let go of tremendous amounts of past trauma and grief as we paved the way to a beautiful future where she could be more peacefully present. My dear friend's transformation was so great in the area we were focused on, that those processes quickly merged into every aspect of her life which gave her the support and tools she needed to blossom into the best and happiest version of herself. After working with her professionally, I quickly realized the power of what life coaching could do.

Did you go through the difficulties that you now help people with? Tell us about that and how it led you to become a coach.

When I got married, I went from being a single mother of one to being a mother of four. These little lives weighed heavily upon me, and I had no idea how to reach a hurting child, let alone care for and nurture four children mainly by myself as my husband built the success of his own company to support us. I knew the pains of being in a split family, being the youngest of five children. The tools and techniques that I learned as a life coach were precisely what I needed to establish harmony in my own home with a family of six very different people.

Before working with and becoming a life coach, I had no idea if I was going to survive another day. Now, I care for all four children as I giddily look forward to what another day will bring. The chaos has not stopped, but I learned how to navigate through my and my family's emotions to start a conversation guided to a real solution. Children's voices must be heard, and their feelings must be addressed. Teaching children how to process their emotions through trials, offers a more prosperous and happy future. This is the main reason I also offer my coaching services to children, and why I believe in coaching so strongly.

If someone were fearful of coaching, what would you tell them?

Coaching has given me the most peace, happiness, and satisfaction in a shorter time than any therapist/counselor has ever given me over the course of years. If you're apprehensive to get a life coach, remember that your health/peace has everything to do with the daily life you live which is deserving of prosperity and happiness. Even as a country, we have not adequately addressed "mental health" or been trained on the severity of healing an unstable mind. A sufficient curriculum is lacking when teaching our children how to deal with their emotions and feelings. Preparation and support when life seems too hard are what our world is missing for both children and adults, but life coaches bridge that gap.

The most significant gift that I can give any of my clients is the gift of releasing old, negative emotions that are holding people back from a life they truly wish to have. Targeting the weight and gloom of trauma in the unconscious mind and freeing every part with respect, love, and release, has been the key to every client's blissful and attainable future. I know the overwhelming feeling, but now I specialize in something far greater than what can keep us down and feeling lost, and that is how to break through all those painful emotions to let the light of a new future shine brightly through.

What would you tell someone that thinks they should be able to fix/solve this on their own?

Human beings are socially tied to each other. Whether we choose to be an asset or a problem, it can affect the central foundation of every life that each person touches. Everyone needs to have a healthy and robust support system, but that is not the case in our world. Circumstances and resources can hinder our ability to solve issues with ease, which can create anger and confusion. However, if we choose to call upon people who specialize in the parts of our life that we do not specialize in, we strengthen our foundation and increase our chances of success and happiness.

How has being a coach and guiding others to empowerment influenced and changed your life?

For many years, I did not know how to control my emotions or manage them adequately and effectively. After becoming a life coach, I found a renewed excitement for life finding value in the present while planning a glorious future. I honestly did not even know what was possible until I worked with a life coach myself! I am thankful for the tools, knowledge, and resources, which are offered in life coaching as a parent/business owner/wife. Having the ability to give back hope to the hopeless and find those who are lost is an empowering feeling. I found true happiness in not hiding behind my pain and being the change that I wanted to see.

What would you tell someone who may have a calling to be a coach?

Life coaches are like doctors; no two are the same or possess the same set of expert skill set, but all are essential. Each life coach brings their own life skills and testimony to be offered for the healing process. All types of life coaches are essential in the present world as no two problems are alike. There is no fakeness in coaching, no "blanket" approach that covers all areas of the topic. Instead, there are specific life coaches whose goals are not just to reach any audience but to tailor skills for each coach to assist every area of concern. If becoming a life coach speaks to you in any way, there is a strong reason, and hesitation will only hinder the greatness of empowerment.

Are there a few steps or tips that you can give someone right now to start them on their transformation?

I believe the best first step to a transformation is to love yourself. There is great power in knowing and loving yourself just the way God made you. We are all striving to be our best selves and be reminded that perfection is not necessary to be a contributing part. You are worthy of more love than you could ever imagine, and as you breathe more life into these words, you will start to live them with ease and grace, which is the best first step to any transformation.

Do you have a gift/session that you can offer us?

In this awesome gift, you can access the tools and strategies to be your best self even when chaos strikes. To unlock these five secrets, simply go to **www.PamperYourProblems.com** and click on the button to access your gift. Do not forget to take advantage of your free 40-minute clarity call with Coach Nikki and start making today so awesome that yesterday gets jealous!

About the Author

Nikki Richmond

Nikki Richmond is the Founder and CEO of Pamper Your Problems. She has mastered breaking down barriers in a loving, compassionate way, which gives all her clients a feeling of joyful weightlessness. After receiving her coaching, clients feel freed from the clutches of stressors that cause them daily anxiety, fear, fatigue, or physical pain. Instead, there is relief combined with an elated excitement for their future, where direction is clear, and possibilities are endless.

Through targeting trauma, pain, anxiety, and fear in my own personal battles, she's learned how to be the calm in the storm. She collaborates with children, parents, business owners, and more, to overcome obstacles while bringing back feelings of hope in the midst of chaos or misdirection.

The Success of You

By Neefah Smith

"You're The Success of You and Success is Full of the Hidden Gemz Within You"

Tell us about yourself, your expertise, and your coaching niche.

Helping others is my passion, motivation is my expertise, and building confidence in clients to unleash their hidden gems is my drive. I am a mother, friend, and coach who receives joy in being of service to family, friends, clients, and others for motivation, inspiration, and support. I am a life and motivational coach who partners with women to become empowered, motivated, and encouraged in reconnecting and rebuilding their relationship with themselves and in unleashing their greatness to move forward in life.

Tell us, what does coaching mean to you?

Coaching brings me the joy and excitement of working with amazing women. At the same time, they bloom at their own pace, unleashing those hidden gems that God has tucked away in their hearts by offering motivation, inspiration, and support one step at a time. My goal is to assist women in bridging the gap and painting the picture of the dreams and goals clients have envisioned for their lives. To be the coach who is willing to take that journey with their clients is simply amazing because when the client wins, whether it is big or small, the coach feels their wins as well. Coaching, teaching, and

71

sharing information with clients watching as they walk into their transformation of what success means to them; what else can a coach ask for? Coaching positions me in a place of service for those clients who need that motivation and support. Our life experiences shape our lives and our relationships. Coaching gives me my heart's desire to see other women win and succeed and walk the path of success they choose for their lives.

What kind of problems do you solve? Can you tell us a bit about the process that you walk people through?

Many clients I have worked with had lost confidence, motivation, and inspiration over the years due to their deteriorating relationship with themselves. Some women lose touch and sight of who they are because they put the needs of children, family, and partners above and before their needs. And when no one is returning the emotional support they need, they become lost, tired, and uninspired by life. We focus on confidence, boundaries, and commitments to ourselves. This process prepares and guides clients to begin walking in their own shoes and choosing the path, dreams, or goals they set for their lives. This guiding technique helps rebuild their relationship with themselves to become successful in various areas of their lives. I share with clients seven hidden gems that will inspire them to embrace limitless possibilities.

I also have an additional technique and process that I use and share with clients. It is called a walk-talk-release! It is a beautiful conversation with God that will lead you on the path that has been hidden in your heart. When you take time out to give yourself what you need, we begin to realize that success means many different things to everyone, but true success for you begins with your mental, emotional, spiritual, and physical well-being. It is a beautiful and powerful movement to realize that everyone holds the key to success in their heart and mind and I am there to assist and support clients in the unleashing of you're the success of you and success is in the becoming.

Do you have a story about a client and how they achieved success with your coaching? Please give details.

Client Johnson was experiencing an emotional roller coaster of rapid waves. Life challenges and obstacles were causing her emotions to flow up and down like the waves of the ocean with rough currents. The wellness of her family was heavy on her heart, and on top of that, she was trying to advance her career with her employer of 10 years. However, it seems like every time she would apply for a promotion, she would receive the generic email, "we have chosen to go with another candidate, etc." That caused Client Johnson to become down on herself, losing confidence in herself and her abilities. She began telling me there was an open position she thought of applying for but felt she was not 100% qualified for because of the previous rejection letters. I encouraged her to post for the job with a new and fresh outlook on herself and her abilities. I asked her to share with me the path her life could take by applying for the position and what if that life were obtainable. That question filled her with hope, encouragement, and excitement.

Client Johnson shared with me in her own words. "Neefah's words of encouragement and her living out her dreams and balancing life, school, family, faith, and her job made me feel that this powerful woman can manage all this. I can surely do one thing and apply for this open position. She is genuine and makes you feel like you are the only person at that moment and her focus and desire for your success are solely on you. She is an excellent coach because she is real. She openly shares her story, her previous challenges that you cannot help but step out and walk towards your dreams and goals. She encouraged me to apply for the position because she knew I had what it took to perform well in that role. Anyone with Neefah as a coach is very fortunate because it is about you and only you. Her motivation and inspiration led me to apply for the open position. By the way! I got the promotion!"

Did you go through the difficulties that you now help people with? Tell us about that and how it led you to become a coach?

Before becoming a life coach, I walked in the circles of life by repeating yesterday's current day's steps. On the inside, I felt that I simply could not take another heartbreak or disappointment in life; I got in a fight with life, and life seemed to be winning, but the hope that was placed within me since day one simply wasn't going to let me take a loss like that. I began going on walks to clear my mind, and one day, I pulled out my phone and began audio journaling. Then one day, my audio recordings began having titles. It took months before I realized I was writing a book. I had so much to share my heart, thoughts, and emotions. The more I talked and exhaled, the more I was releasing pain, and the more I inhaled Joy, happiness, confidence, and self-love were filling me up. After repeatedly listening to the audio recordings, I remember saying, " OMG, these are my conversations with God and other ladies." That is how I began the walk talk release process sharing my heart with God, but He was teaching and preparing me to become a coach and counselor along the way.

If someone were fearful of coaching? What would you tell them?

It is perfectly normal to be fearful or nervous or have anxiety about doing something that goes against the norm in our lives and inviting new people into our life is no different. Think of your coach as your personal cheerleader and guide that will support you in clarifying, and setting achieving goals every step of the way, while creating strategies to bypass obstacles and challenges that may have been holding a person back. And at the end of the day, think of your coach as a great friend who only wants to see you succeed and go further in life.

What would you tell someone that thinks they should be able to fix/solve this on their own?

One of the greatest lessons I have learned in life is that we all need love, guidance, and support on our journey, and there is power in the connection of sisterhood of the coach and client. Use your strengths and lean on your coach for a fresh new perspective of ideas and new techniques on how to break down goals to achieve them step by step. One day I thought: what if God is the cloud and we the people are the rain and God sprinkles us on earth to love and support one another. We do not have to go through life trying to fix or solve all our problems independently. The power of connections pushes us forward.

How has being a coach and guiding others to empowerment influenced and changed your life?

Coaching has shown me how much I have evolved in so many areas of my life. Since I was sixteen and a single mother, I have been on my own. Those challenging times and obstacles of life prepared me to be one of the dopest coaches in life. I had to walk through those obstacles in life to heal, evolve, and receive the lessons, so when I collaborate with clients, I am sharing my heart, thoughts, and emotions coming from a place of wholeness. When I see clients evolving and, on the path, to walking in their purpose, it gives me a sense of joy and excitement to be walking in my purpose of coaching. Every technique I support and walk through with a client is a step and plan that God has walked me through.

What would you tell someone who may have a calling to be a coach?

YESSS, Go For it! The power is in the coaching to share your story of overcoming, evolving, and unleashing success in your area of expertise. Life lessons are blessings, and blessings are meant to be shared with others. There is always someone who needs to hear your story for encouragement, motivation, and inspiration because we all have scars, and God has a way of turning scars into shining stars to show others just how bright they can shine.

Are there a few steps or tips that you can give someone right now to start them on their transformation?

Yes, we all need healthy coping mechanisms. So, I would suggest incorporating the walk-talk-release method into your life.

- **Walking is movement, and movement brings energy and creativity, and innovation.** It is a form of meditation that brings anyone into the present moment taking in all the surrounding inspiration in life.

- **Talking, having a conversation with God or audio journal helps everyone rediscover who they are, their wants, dreams/goals.** It helps practice positive self-talk, which leads to confidence in who they are, and it is a great way to work on one of the best relationships you or anyone will ever have in life, the relationship with you.

- **Releasing is something magical or powerful, whatever you choose to call it.** When you release the pain and hurt by walking and talking one step at a time, you allow God to take all that pain, hurt, and burdens you have been carrying and turn them into joy, happiness, thankfulness, and gratitude, and Godfidence.

So, when you combine the walk-talk-release process, know you are on the best journey of your life.

Do you have a gift/session that you can offer us?

Please go to my website, **www.HiddenGemzCoaching.com**, to download the "*7 Hidden Gemz of Investing in You*" workbook.

About the Author

Neefah Smith

Neefah Smith, currently lives in Greensboro NC with her daughter Aniya. Neefah is a motivational speaker, coach, and author. She is a certified Life Coach and owner of Hidden Gemz Coaching LLC and the creator of You're the Success of You. Neefah is the author of Walk Talk Release Conversations with God and God's Pathway, along with Journaling the Journey Workbook. She is currently pursuing a degree in Psychology to become a Licensed Professional Counselor. Her goal is to partner with women to become "Successful & Empowered", while building Confidence, Inspiration, and Motivation one step at a time. Coach Neefah journey began on a walk releasing and audio journaling her thoughts, heart and emotions sharing conversations with God, which lead on a path of healing, wholeness and self-discovery, motivation, and inspiration one step at a time. Coach Neefah believes every woman has hidden gemz within and is ready to be unleashed into Success.

Choose You

By Dr. Maria Simard

"To be beautiful means to be yourself. You do not need to be accepted by others. You need to accept yourself."
~ Thich Nhat Hanh

Tell us about yourself, your expertise, and your coaching niche.

Aloha! Maria here...aka Priestess Ria Big Girl Diva. Body Love Recovery Doula, Transformational Intuitive Healer, Soul Whisperer, and all-around Witchy Vibe Giving Woman. I am on a mission to liberate and emancipate "big girls," "fat chicks," and dimpled thighed women everywhere. Ending their body hatred stories and supporting them on their journey of recovery in self-love, self-expression, and sacred sensuality.

Tell us, what does coaching mean to you?

Coaching to me is a partnership. A sacred contract even. It is a forward-facing do with process that helps someone get from where they are to where they want to be. It provides support and accountability on the path to achieving an outcome, completing a goal, and getting a specific result. It is an invaluable tool to use.

What kind of problems do you solve? Can you tell us a bit about the process that you walk people through?

As for me, I offer a bit more than coaching in its basic definition. You see, the body remembers everything - every strong emotion you have ever had, every story you have ever told yourself, and how other people, places, and things have made you feel are held in the cellular makeup of your body. This can weigh you down. If you are having a tough time reducing physical weight and have tried everything and more, you may have such a stored-in story. Until you let it go. Release it, detox, and recover. Magical things happen when you can see your beauty, love your body, heal your heart and be your bootayy-licious self. You can be, do, and have all the joy, love, intimacy, orgasms, and cha-ching you want from this space and place. Every woman's story is unique; each process to healing and recovery is a deeply personal one.

Do you have a story about a client and how they achieved success with your coaching? Please give details.

I remember spending time with Kimmie. Kimmie was in recovery from alcohol addiction; she would be on the wagon and off the wagon several times a month. She wanted to start an online business, so she came to see me. And as you can probably guess, she was on again and off again with the work she needed to do to start her business. We had one of those tough conversations about commitment. She burst out in tears... "I am not a quitter! I never quit anything!"
BOOM! There it was... the story, the intense emotion, and the language pattern.

I said, "Kimmie, may I ask you something? What does I am not a quitter mean to you?"

For over an hour, she shared stories about her parents and things they would say. I do not think she had ever been able to let those things out before. When she finished,

I said, "Kimmie, may I ask you another question? Do you want to quit drinking?"

She said, "Yes, of course."

I replied, "What would happen when you let go of "I am not a quitter! I never quit anything!"

A few aha-induced superlatives later... she got it. She had to loosen up her grip on being a quitter to quit drinking for good. Everything changed for Kimmie that day, as it did for me too.

Did you go through the difficulties that you now help people with? Tell us about that and how it led you to become a coach?

I have been a big girl in hiding for most of my life. I spent so much time, energy, and other resources to just not be big anymore. It was exhausting and soul-crushing. I would be the girl at the event that you could not find in pictures because either I took the photos to purposely avoid them, or I ducked in behind someone or something. I had been shamed, ridiculed, bullied, overlooked, and abused by other people and myself. No more! Not for me, and not for you either. I have not always listened to the gentle whispers of spirit. Sometimes it took multiple body slams to my Root Chakra for me to catch on. Today and at this moment, I am listening. I know now without any doubt who it is I am here to look after. And I know with laser lucid clarity what I am here to share, teach, and help heal up!

What makes you different from other coaches? (Uniqueness)

Differentiating from the masses comes down to one thing. Be you, and you cannot duplicate that now, can you? LOL! To summarize my values or "essence of being," as I like to say. I CARE! Integrity, Connection, Aloha, Respect, and Empathy. The ability to hold sacred space, hear at a soul level, and unconditionally serve from love, peace, and divine energy. To feel seen, heard, and acknowledged from where you are right now. I love that and work to embody that every moment.

If someone were fearful of coaching, what would you tell them?

Coaching is fantastic, and advantageous and can help you get results if you want to accomplish a specific goal or outcome. The support and accountability you will get from coaching can be the difference that makes the difference. I highly recommend it.

Now, I will caution you. Not all coaches are created equal. The industry has undergone many changes over the years. Please spend some time exploring and learning about the person/company you are thinking of having a coaching relationship with before you invest. The investment in yourself is totally worth it. Make sure your investment in them is too!

What would you tell someone that thinks they should be able to fix/solve this on their own?

I am a firm believer in that you have everything you need already inside you, and that everything you want to be, do, and have is waiting for you to receive it. With that being said, we do not always know how to draw it out, what to do with it or where to look. I also know that motivation is fickle, and procrastination is most folks' middle name. It is ok to ask for help, especially from folks who are further down the path than you are. You can save yourself a lot of time, energy, and resources in getting there.

How has being a coach and guiding others to empowerment influenced and changed your life?

Learning through the empowerment of others has been fundamental in my growth as a transformational servant and leader. Being of service to those around me has taught me volumes beyond my tiny little sample of the universe. More than my Doctoral studies ever did. People are incredible, our minds are magical, and our souls are thirsty for love and transformation. I love witnessing people "try on" new ways of thinking, seeing, and feeling. It gifts me with learnings and fuels my desire to grow and create a much more significant impact on the world. I am humbled each day and honored by those who choose to allow me to be their guide.

What would you tell someone who may have a calling to be a coach?

So, you want to coach, that is awesome.
It is a rewarding and a not without hard work call to service

Consider these questions if you would...

- Why do you want to coach?
- What does being a coach mean to you?
- What do you think your life will look, feel and be like as a coach?

Do your internal work. This really is a non-negotiable step.

Model and train with someone you resonate with. Take your time choosing a mentor. Ignore the flashy websites and comparison of what others in the industry are saying. And lastly, the world does not need another URL. It needs your service. Go forth and be a change maker.

Are there a few steps or tips that you can give someone right now to start them on their transformation?

Here are a few tips to keep in mind:

1. **Go easy on yourself**. There is no right way or wrong way to heal up or get to your destination. Enjoy the joy IN the journey.
2. **Comparison is a killer.** Just do not do it. There will always be someone with a skill set, natural or learned talent, more AND less than your own. That is just how it is.
3. **Know what your values are.** Do not just guess what you think they might or should be. Re-evaluate over time. What is important to you can and will change based on where you are on your path.
4. **A' Ohe pau ka 'ikei ka halau ho 'okahi** - Not all knowledge is learned in one school.
5. **And lastly... you got this!** Crawl if you must; just keep going. You are worthy, and You are enough.

Do you have a gift/session that you can offer us?

Thank you for reading my chapter. Please accept this small gift, *"There is Magick in You"* Planner and Journal. You can access your gift on my website: **www.BigGirlDiva.co**

About the Author

Dr. Maria Simard

Dr. Maria Simard "aka" Priestess Ria Big Girl Diva is a Concierge Sacred Sensuality & Body Love Recovery Doula and Creatrix of The Divine Diva Detox. She is on a mission to liberate and emancipate her fellow big girl divas from the decades of shame, guilt and grief that is stored in the cells of their body. As a Big Girl Diva for most of her adult life she has come to realize that you must ditch the body hatred stories to stand unapologetically in your divine femme power. Gifted and skilled in various modalities Maria has an unprecedented understanding that each woman has a unique story and each woman's healing journey is different. Her ability to hold sacred space, listen/hear at a soul level, and serve as a guide to get you to and through the root of the matter is her superpower.

Soar to Success

By Devette Wright

Tell us about yourself, your expertise, and your coaching niche.

My name is Devette Anderson, also known as Coach Dee. I am a divorcee from a 25-year marriage that failed, and I decided to transcend into a successful single woman and a mother of 2 wonderful sons. I'm also a woman of prayer, a servant leader, a certified professional life coach, motivational speaker, author, and publisher. Amid this pandemic, I created an online community called S.O.A.R.E.R.S. A faith-based organization designed for broken women that find themselves stuck in life due to adversities and traumatic experiences. S.O.A.R.E.R.S. LLC is also my coaching business where I assist others in strategizing opportunities to allow a total to live an amazing life.

Tell us, what does coaching mean to you?

Coaching is effectively serving others and helping them through goal setting to succeed. It is my purpose, passion, and privilege. In my everyday experiences coaching, I have learned that coaching has a dual role, how to become empowered and soar that I may teach others that there is hope and as they put in the work, they can do the same. As I listen to their hearts, I can locate where they are (spiritually/emotionally) and begin to encourage them by sharing with them that there is an answer, and the good news is that it is within them. They hold the key, and God has given me wisdom and power to teach them how to use it through coaching as we lock and unlock those doors to their freedom.

What kind of problems do you solve? Can you tell us a bit about the process that you walk people through?

As a coach, I realize I am also a solutionist. I always find myself presented with emotionally wounded people and desire healing, stuck and desire to transcend, empty and desire to be filled, rejected and want to be accepted, and those who are aimlessly walking through life merely existing feeling hopeless and insignificant. These were the traits (and mindsets) of the woman I once was, and my healing was a process. Above all the detours in my life, including the trauma from divorce, I have the power of prayer, meditation, and serving others. As a life coach, I understand that this is case by case and may vary depending on the person's particular situation and expectations.

I believe my personality, my Godfidence (confidence in God), my southern charm, and simply my authenticity as I freely share my stories with others that are divinely appointed for me make me unique. I know that I am a miracle, and I have the power within me to produce others.

Do you have a story about a client and how they achieved success with your coaching? Please give details.

Ms. Cee is a client/ mentee whom I had the opportunity to assist during her transition from a place of being stuck to soaring. Today, she is evolving in every area of her life! It has been amazing to witness her metamorphosis. A few years ago, I met this young lady in the workplace. When I saw her, I began to reminisce and reflect on where I once was. As I looked into her eyes to focus on her broken soul and hear the cry from her heart, all I felt was humility and compassion. I immediately knew she was an assignment, and God prepared me to serve her. I learned she was traumatized from her youth and was transitioning from her life as she knew it, from marriage to separation with two children. I knew her life would never be the same and I assured her that no matter what the outcome would be, she absolutely could but being intentional to take the necessary steps was paramount to her healing process. I encouraged her to give herself permission to feel and acknowledge where she was (spiritually, mentally, emotionally, physically, financially, etc.).

As an overcomer, a visionary, and a life coach, I understand that if you are going to rediscover who you truly are, self-awareness, self-actualization, and self-mastery are all crucial to healing. I also taught her that forgiving herself and then others were a factor. During our sessions, I would listen as she emptied herself. Afterward, I would begin to share specific techniques that would help her throughout her journey, such as the value of deep breathing, meditation, journaling her thoughts, renewing her mind through positive, life-giving words of affirmation, recognizing her triggers, setting boundaries, and of course, setting goals. Even if you are afraid, you can still take steps in faith because it is the antidote to conquering fear. Over time, I have watched Ms. Cee Cee's confidence arise and her life transform. Today, she has been reintroduced to herself and allows God to restore her in every area of her life. During this pandemic, she took this as an opportunity to invest in herself by furthering her education. Ms. Cee enrolled in college to become a business owner. She is a great example of one who has learned to soar as she strategizes opportunities to allow a total restoration. Ms. Cee is preparing to graduate this year!

Did you go through the difficulties that you now help people with? Tell us about that and how it led you to become a coach?

Yes, I did go through the difficulties, as I have shared, but the difference is that I made (and I still make) a decision to come out. This is how I can tap into the power of coaching others. When I was introduced to coaching, I functioned in it, but I had no idea until it was revealed. Serving others is who I am naturally. It is my purpose, and nothing is more rewarding to me than helping others.

If someone were fearful of coaching, what would you tell them?

I meet men and women who think about coaching but are afraid to move forward. I politely remind them of who they are. They are the solution to someone's problem, and the world needs their gifts, abilities, and talents. There is someone longing to be launched into their next desire the coach explicitly created for them.

What would you tell someone that thinks they should be able to fix/solve this on their own?

Over these past few years, it has always been someone coming along my side coaching that has propelled me to become the best version of myself to ensure that I am effective as I share with others.

Knowing my potential has also caused me to produce fruit and not procrastinate. I would tell them to try getting a coach! I'm proof that the power of having a coach does work.

How has being a coach and guiding others to empowerment influenced and changed your life?

For personal development, it simply caused me to become the best version of myself, which I always offer to others.

What would you tell someone who may have a calling to be a coach?

To that individual who has the inclination that they have been called to be a coach, I say unto you that it is my prayer that you would answer the call with a complete yes.

Do you have a gift/session that you can offer us?

Yes, I would like to offer you a 30-minute session with me. Simply go to my website to access your gift: **www.Strength2Soar.com.**

About the Author

Devette M. Wright

Devette Wright is a woman of great faith and fortitude with a zeal for prayer and a mandate for intercession. Coach Dee, as she is affectionately called, is a warrior and no stranger to the detours in life you may be traveling. she is very passionate and committed to helping others grow in prayer. Through her work as a Published Author, Public Speaker, and Certified Life Coach she strives to help others reclaim their lives. Devette is also a student at Impact University School of Prayer and a servant leader in the renowned DWU (Divorced Women Unite) where she was the recipient of the 2021 Pinnacle award. Coach Dee has been instrumental in the personal development of many for years which led to creating SOARER'S Facebook Group (women only). As a Life Coach, Devette offers services designed to prepare individuals from all walks of life to soar. Her purpose is to teach others how to pray and share her journey teaching those in need in both spiritual and practical ways to believe in themselves and to walk in confidence. Her mission is simply to serve others and make an impact that will help add value to their lives.

Coaching Empowers You

By Ronjeanna Harris

Tell us about yourself, your expertise, and your coaching niche.

Ronjeanna Harris nurse, award-winning wellness coach, published author, educator, motivational speaker, and kingdom warrior. I specialize in natural skincare products and services. I am carefully formulating products for hair and body— skilled and experienced LPN with over 20 years in the healthcare field. I am the unorthodox wellness coach that ignites and charges your accountability. I educated the client in wellness fundamentals by customizing programs and/or sessions tailored to the focused goal. I love God, and I am an ambassador of God in the marketplace and coaching. My role as wife, mother, and grandma is a priority. I love my family. They keep me balanced.

Tell us, what does coaching mean to you?

Coaching is a very vital resource that has a profound impact well-properly implemented. This strategy creates the goal of execution for the individual obtaining services. Coaching is essential; Coaching enhances structure and discipline. Coaching gives the client encouragement to keep moving forward. This technique has been remarkably successful, along with helping the clients find the answer to their concern. Coaching heals as well. This amazing area of service is uniquely diverse. Guidance is given by allowing the client to be in control to pull the purpose to the surface. Society, life, this pandemic has ignited creatives to branch out in unique ways, and having coaching helps their journey become successful. Lifestyle changes for the better get accomplished through the coach services. This service provides clarity in many areas.

Hope gets restored through coaching. This also creates a healthier community. People find answers that have been on the inside of them that shock them and motivate them. Coaching means the impact of solutions. The world gets enhanced movement of flow in purpose through coaching igniting—the heaviness of not knowing how, gets released to better focus. Strategic utilization of coaching is so powerful. A dynamic way to serve. Its purpose saving to the client in more cases. I love serving in this sector in wellness. I love the growth that gets demonstrated with coaching. Purpose gets birthed or rebirthed with the assistance of the coach. Often clarity is refined within the client(s). This strategy is so amazing to witness. I was a coach and have coaches/mentors because I want to fulfill my God-assigned purpose in excellence. Assistance to great intentional acceleration is good sound ground for a dynamic win.

What kind of problems do you solve? Can you tell us a bit about the process that you walk people through?

Kingdom Solutionist is a faith-based coaching and mentoring service that assists clients in wellness or the beauty sector in business. We service individuals looking to build and/or start their business in the industry. We focus on the safe scope of practice and the fundamental education on the proper operation of skincare and wellness through mentorship. The goal of coaching is to provide clarify-driven tactics to aid the client in identifying the solution to their goal or concern. We created a structured plan of action with smart goals. We also apply faith-based principles, so we believe in leading the holy spirit even in business. Each potential client goes through a consultation assessment process before giving the option the retain us for services. This way, we identify that we are an effective fit for the need or services expressed. We analyze what level the client is at to build out sessions and customize programs for the individual properly. According to the target focus, there may also be perks of training and free courses to enhance further build and cultivate proper execution of the client goal.

Do you have a story about a client and how they achieved success with your coaching? Please give details.

One successful testimony of our services is the massage therapist that inquired about services to structure and launch a skincare business. The client had nothing established and wanted to get to a goal to launch a business and have products available in e-commerce. We design a customized 3-month program to prepare them for an effective introduction to the world during the pandemic. They got insightful knowledge and were able to launch a top-notch online natural skincare business that was able to thrive in a time of the unknown because of Covid19. The success of execution for the client was the most rewarding part of our guided service. This is what it is all about, the impact of solutions. I will say this often because that is what the coach assists with when servicing clients.

Did you go through the difficulties that you now help people with? Tell us about that and how it led you to become a coach?

I encountered so many hurdles in the business's wellness and natural skincare journey. I did not come to the scene successfully at the beginning of launching. Just Jeanna's Skin Care was birthed with amazing products; however, I did not have a good structure on the business side. I did not have mentorship or coaching guidance in the beginning. So, there were several moments of trial and error. When I faced a few of those trials and errors, it eventually ignites an evaluation of the business. I had a phenomenal gift and was off to a good start, but there was no grounded structure. I needed guidance from a like-minded business owner that was thriving in the direction of the path God had given me for my business. I experienced rejection at the beginning of my journey to the business world when first seeking mentorship guidance. If you are not strong enough, it can get discouraging, but that cannot be an area to entertain because you will lose valued time that could enhance continue building out of your business.

I am so glad I invested in getting under the mentorship and having a coach. This decision helps me pivot. This enabled me to work on areas that I was not strong in. I was able to start seeing goals mastered. It is like doors began to open. I got greater confidence as well. My business began to look like a long-term success. My target clients were more visually. So, trials and error helped align me to the position to become the coach I am today.

If someone were fearful of coaching, what would you tell them?

Suppose one may have the desired passion to coach but hesitate or be fearful. First, I suggest seeking God's guidance for direction. Know that fear is often a hindering factor to distract your purpose. Research the coaching area one aims to serve in. Get the necessary training from a structured credential program. Push past fear to fulfill the purpose of helping potential future clients assigned to you. Look into mentoring coaching guidance to groom and develop in serving in this sector. Never let fear be entertained in your life. One potential is more significant than fear. The creativity in one serving as a coach may be the answer to someone's journey. I challenge you to embrace the coaching to pursue coaching. There is a great need and the more that align to help others through serving in expertise, the better the community, economy, and so much more. Never doubt your ability to impact.

What would you tell someone that thinks they should be able to fix/solve this on their own?

I always let people know that having a team is essential. Never think that you must face circumstances and/or life situations independently. Therefore, coaches like me, and many others have taken to stand to serve and help others find and master solutions effectively.

Challenges should not be faced alone, if possible, especially when one may be at a hard stop and simply may need secure guidance in life journey. There are times of regrouping, but in the case of finding purposeful solutions to goals, coaching often is necessary to help accountability and consistency.

How has being a coach and guiding others to empowerment influenced and changed your life?

Serving as a coach has been such a rewarding accomplishment. To contribute to helping others pursue and execute goals on purpose is a blessing. It is like helping ignite more problem solvers in the world. We can never have too many of them. God is glorified by seeing His children helping others in different areas of coaching. This experience journey of my life has been impactful. I love serving, so this ignited my passion even more. It is seeing the results of impact. It amazes me in so many ways.

What would you tell someone who may have a calling to be a coach?

If you have been called to this area, yield to obedience and get certified to operate in your calling. The bible says in Hebrews 3:15 "when you hear my voice harden not your heart." Move into the mission. Prepare for it. Settle in it. Be excited about it. Look at it this way, do not hold up someone's destiny from one not being in position. Nothing is perfect at first. There may be moments of defining your purpose but proceed forward to make a significant difference. Do not second guess it. Oh, course, pray, plan, prepare to serve effectively.

Are there a few steps or tips that you can give someone right now to start them on their transformation?

Steps to start igniting the journey

1. Prayer
2. Research
3. Education of the coaching area you are looking to serve it
4. Sit down with an advisor for insight guidance
5. Create an outline projection to launch into coaching
6. Research the statistics and areas of need
7. Attend workshops and seminars in your local area
8. Seek mentoring and or internship to learn and build skill

Do you have a gift/session that you can offer us?

Enjoy a 20 min consultation with me. Simply contact me on my website at **www.JustJeannas.com**

About the Author

Ronjeanna Harris

Ronjeanna Harris is a God fearing chosen ordain Evangelist, affirmed Prophet & Intercessor. Ronjeanna also is a wife, mother of 6 and grandmother. This game changer is the proud owner of Just Jeanna's Skin Care LLC. Natural Product creator & Formulator launch company in 2018 after much prayer, research, and preparation. After just 2 years in business, Just Jeanna's Skin Care LLC got approved to be in the Walmart marketplace in 2020. Ronjeanna is a Published Author, LPN & award-winning Certified Wellness Coach with over 20 years of experience & skill in the healthcare industry. Just Jeanna's Skin Care LLC offers a host of services to clients locally, national, and international. This trailblazer in May 2021 started her own nonprofit organization Jeanna's iFeed doing what she loves which is being a servant. Kingdom Solutionist coaching & mentoring services was birthed in 2021. Community serving and giving back is an honor and passion for Ronjeanna. Providing natural wellness solutions is Ronjeanna mission to stand by.

What's Next?

Lean In. Let Go. Leap Forward.

What did you think of the stories and expertise that our authors had to share?

Did you learn a few new things that you can take back to your life or work?

Do you now have a better understanding of the power of coaching and how it can be an incredible avenue for transformation in your life and the lives of others?

Did it motivate you to consider being a coach or leveling up as one to facilitate deeper transformations for all those around you?

My hope is that you have a fresh new way of thinking about the coaching industry. If so, please go over to Amazon and leave us a 5-star review!

Our authors were hand-selected for their level of expertise, genuine integrity, and overall level of achievement in the coaching industry. If you enjoyed reading some of their stories and learning about how they help their clients, please take the next step, and reach out to those who inspired you.

Most of the authors in this book speak to groups of all sizes, both in-person and virtually. They also offer products, programs, events, and services that can support you in your life, health, relationships, business/career.

I highly recommend that you take advantage of their special offers, additional downloads, and more when you visit each of the websites listed at the end of their chapters.

In addition, I have put together a website where you can access the author's information to make it easy for you to follow up. There are also more resources on the page about this topic. Go to www.PowerofCoachingBook.com right now, before you forget who you wanted to connect with or find out more about.

Thank you for reading this book. I look forward to bringing you more powerful messages from others in upcoming books, plus more training and teachings in my own books.

If you are interested in becoming an author, have a message to share with the world, and would like to be considered in one of our upcoming books, please go to www.AnotherLevelPublishing.com and apply. Becoming an author in our book collaborations provides many benefits, which you will discover on the website.

Grab One or More of Free Training Now and Take Your Business and Life to Another Level!

Learn:

- The Power of Emotional Intelligence
- The Power of Being a Life Coach
- The Power of Biz/Life Harmony
- 3 Secrets to Mastering the Art of Your Communication
- 5 Secrets to Peace Under Pressure
- Digital Marketing Made Easy
- Using Your Story to Attract More Clients
- And Many More!

Get Access Online at:
www.AnotherLevelLiving.com/FreeTrainings

Want to Become a Life Coach or Level Up as a Coach?

Become a Certified Life Coach &

Emotional Intelligence Expert in Just 4 Days!

This is Our Life Harmony Coach

Certification Training Program

Program Benefits

- Start a coaching business right away or scale a current business.
- Expand your capacity & energy as a leader.
- Provide your clients with deep breakthroughs for lasting change.
- Positive impact on self and others around you.
- Increase confidence, energy, & health.

- Breakthrough obstacles and conflicts.
- Cultivate emotional wisdom.
- Improve communication skills.
- Strengthen relationships with ease.
- Reduce stress and increase profits.
- Business & Marketing Expertise Covered.

Learn More at:
www.AnotherLevelLiving.com/Trainings

Want to Unleash the Power of Your Mind and Show Others How to do the Same?

Become a Certified Mind Expert &

Neuro-Linguistics Programming (NLP) Practitioner in Just 5 Days!

This is Our Communication Mastery

Certification Training Program

Program Benefits

- Resolve Inner Conflicts.
- Increase Your Confidence
- Be Able to Raise Your Prices.
- Break-free from Bad Habits and Limiting Beliefs.
- Operate with More Ease, Grace, & Flow.
- Strengthen Relationships.
- Become the Leader You're Called to Be.
- Gain More Experience & Expertise to Grow Your Biz.

- Facilitate Deeper Transformations.
- Easily Attract & Motivate Your Clients.
- Shift Your Mindset to Receive Your Prosperity.
- Stand Out from Your Competitors.
- Establish Your Own Unique Brand that speaks to your ideal audience.

Learn More at:
www.AnotherLevelLiving.com/Trainings

Made in the USA
Middletown, DE
07 October 2022

12098942R00066